A Sense of Science:
Exploring Electricity

Claire Llewellyn

SEA-TO-SEA
Mankato Collingwood London

This edition first published in 2009 by
Sea-to-Sea Publications
Distributed by Black Rabbit Books
P.O. Box 3263
Mankato, Minnesota 56002

Printed in China

Library of Congress
Cataloging-in-Publication Data:

Llewellyn, Claire.
  Exploring electricity / Claire Llewellyn.
     p. cm. -- (A sense of science)
  Summary: "A simple exploration of electricity
that covers how we use electricity and how it is
made, plus batteries and circuits. Includes
activities"--Provided by publisher.
  Includes bibliographical references and index.
  ISBN 978-1-59771-127-2 (alk. paper)
  1. Electricity--Juvenile literature. I. Title.
  QC527.2.L545 2009
  537--dc22
                              2008007327

9 8 7 6 5 4 3 2

Published by arrangement with the
Watts Publishing Group Ltd, London.

Editor: Jeremy Smith
Art Director: Jonathan Hair
Design: Matthew Lilly
Cover and design concept:
Jonathan Hair
Photography: Ray Moller unless
otherwise stated.

Photograph credits:
Alamy: 10b, 25t,
Corbis: 6, 11t, 13b, 17b.

We would like to thank Scallywags for
their help with the models in this book.

Contents

We use electricity

We use electricity
every day.

We use it when
we turn on a
computer.

We use electricity to turn a stereo on.

Telephones run on electricity.

All electric

Look around you. Can you see something that runs on electricity?

Electric light

Electricity
gives us light.

We turn
on lights when
it gets dark
so we
can see.

Streetlights come on at night.

See the light

With a grown-up, light a candle in the dark. Then switch on an electric light. How are the two lights different?

A car's headlights use electricity.

Electric heat

Electricity gives us heat.

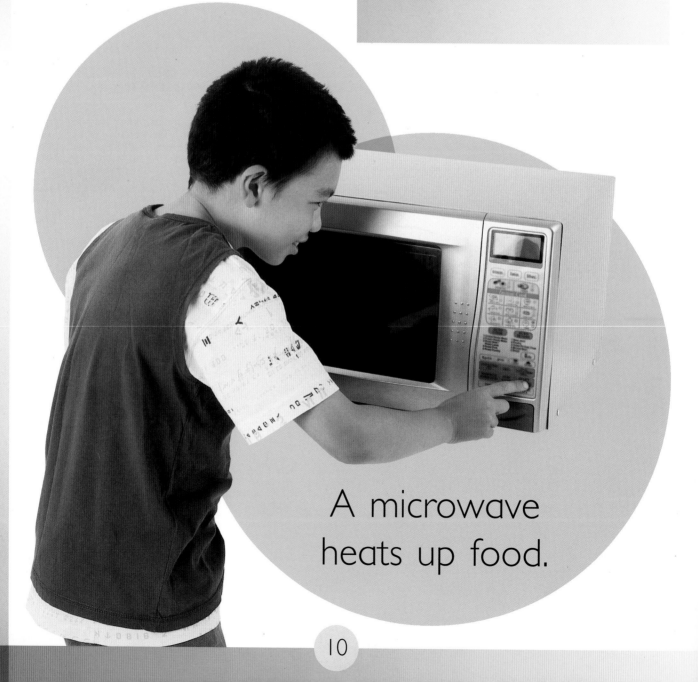

Hot stuff

With an adult, switch on a machine that gives out heat. What changes do you notice? What happens when you turn it off?

A microwave heats up food.

Electricity makes an iron hot.

An electric heater warms up a room.

Electric machines

Many machines run on electricity.

A fan spins around and keeps us cool.

On the move
What happens when you turn on a blow-dryer?
What happens when you switch it off?

A washing machine washes our dirty clothes.

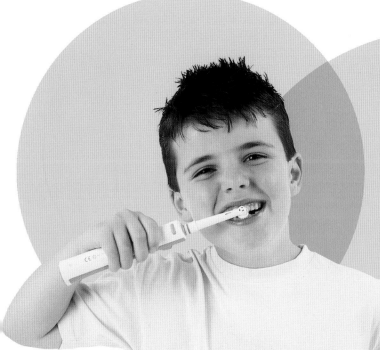

Some people brush their teeth with an electric toothbrush.

Making sound

Some electric
machines can make
sounds.

We can play
music on an
MP3 player.

Loud or soft?

Turn on a radio. What happens?
What can you do to make the sound louder?
How can you make it softer?

We can hear our friend's voice on the telephone.

This keyboard works on electricity.

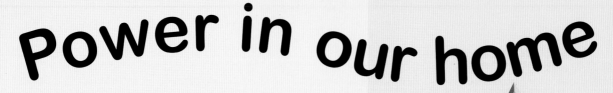

Power in our home

Many electric
machines have
a plug that fits
in an outlet
in the wall.

Electricity
is dangerous.
Never touch
electrical outlets
in the wall.

This vacuum cleaner
uses electricity.

Electricity is made in power plants.

It flows along wires and into our homes.

In the wire

With an adult, look at a piece of electric cord. What can you see inside?

Looking at batteries

Some electric machines run on batteries.

Battery play

Turn a flashlight on and off. Now find the batteries and take them out. What happens when you turn the flashlight on now?

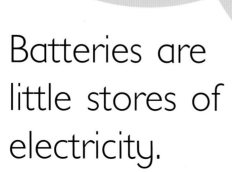

Batteries are little stores of electricity.

When the batteries run out, we put new ones in or recharge the old ones.

Machines with batteries have no cord and are easy to move around.

Making a circuit

Electricity flows along a pathway called a circuit.

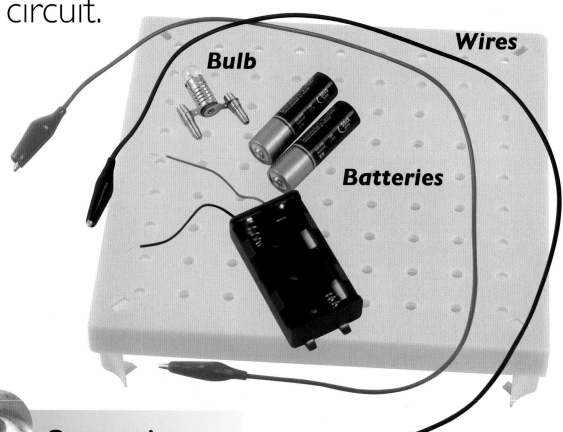

Bulb

Wires

Batteries

Sense box

Look carefully at the lightbulb. Can you see anything inside it?

We can make a circuit with a battery, two wires, and a bulb.

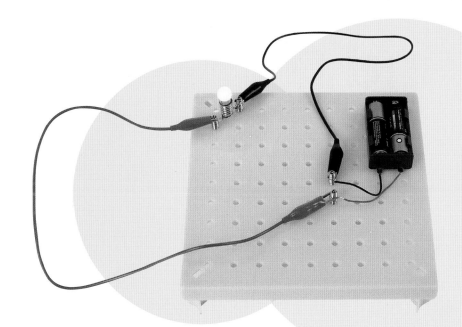

When we join all the parts of the circuit, the bulb lights up.

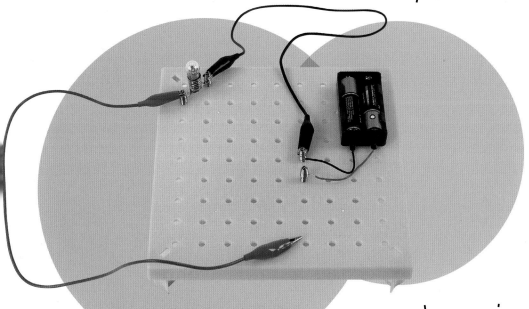

If there is a gap in the circuit, the bulb goes out.

On and off

Electricity flows into a machine when we turn it on.

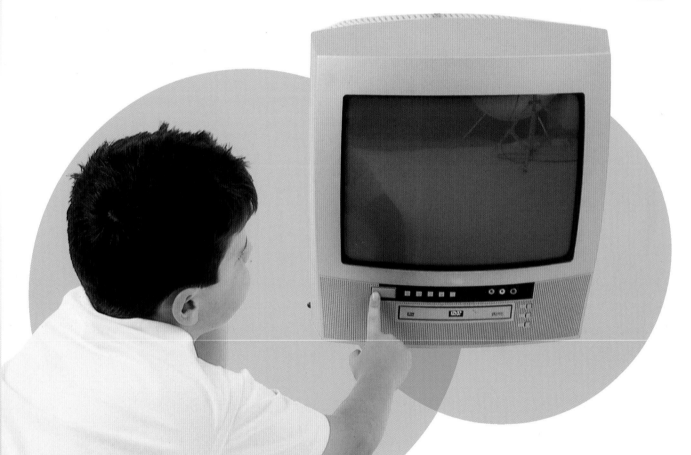

If we push the button, the television switches on.

We press the switch to turn the toy on.

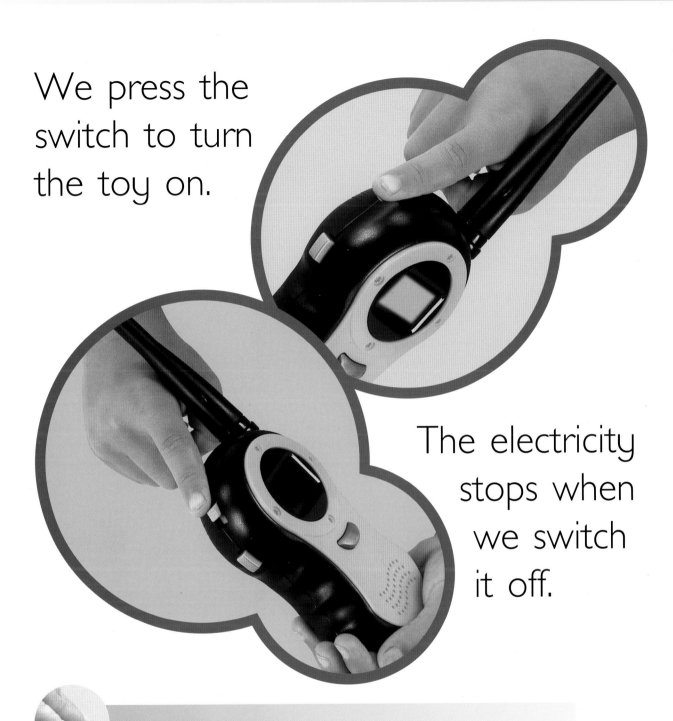

The electricity stops when we switch it off.

Sense box

Have a look in your bathroom.
How do you turn the bathroom light on?
How do you turn it off?

Electrical parts

Electric machines have lots of different parts.

Sense box
Feel a piece of cord with your hands. What does the outside feel like? Do you know what it is made of?

Bulb

Cord

These are the electric parts of a lamp.

These are the electric parts of a flashlight.

Bulb

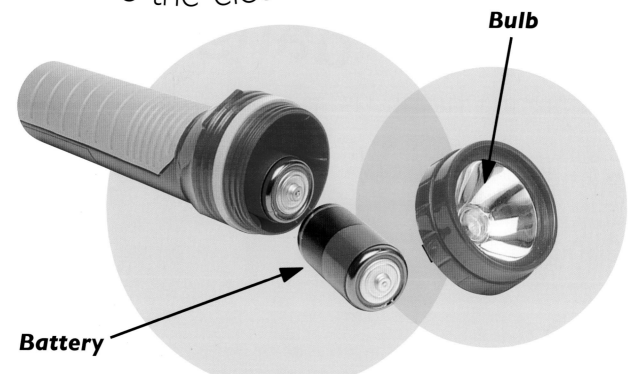

Battery

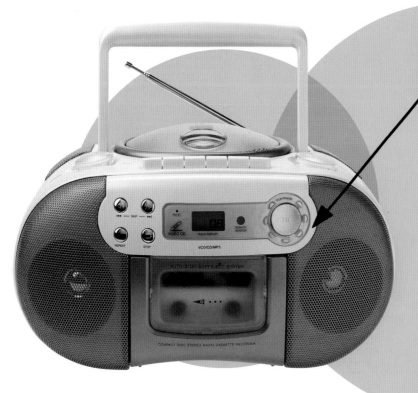

On/Off switch

These are the electric parts of a CD-player.

Electricity is dangerous

Electricity helps us in many ways but it can be very dangerous.

We must never play with plugs, outlets, or wires.

Never play near electricity outside.

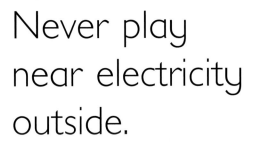

Batteries are the safest way to learn about electricity.

Stay safe

Draw a sketch of your kitchen. Mark the areas where you need to be careful because of electricity.

Glossary

Battery
A portable device that contains electricity.

Bulb
The glass part of an electric lamp that gives out light.

Circuit
A loop that electricity can flow along.

Cord
The flexible wire found on machines that run on electricity.

Outlet
A place in a wall designed for a plug to be inserted to receive electricity.

Power plant
The place where electricity is made.

Plug
A device on an electrical appliance inserted into an outlet to gain electricity.

Switch
Something that starts or stops electricity flowing.

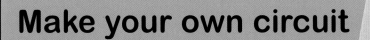

bulb

battery

circuit board

leads

You will need a bulb, circuit board, wires, and a battery.

Set up your circuit to match the one on page 21. Attach each wire to the battery and the bulb.

What happens if you unclip a wire?

Index